Moments with Oneself Series : 16

D1798017

Yoga *of* Objectivity

Swami Dayananda Saraswati
Arsha Vidya

Arsha Vidya Research and Publication Trust
Chennai

Published by :
Arsha Vidya Research and Publication Trust
4 ' Srinidhi ' Apts 3rd Floor
Sir Desika Road Mylapore
Chennai 600 004 INDIA
Tel   : 044 2499 7023, 2499 7131
Email   : avrandpt@gmail.com
Website : www.avrpt.com

ISBN : 978 - 93 - 80049 - 13 - 7

First Edition : January 2010   Copies : 2000
First Reprint : January 2011   Copies : 1000
2nd Reprint : July   2012   Copies : 1000
3rd Reprint   : April   2014   Copies : 1000
4th Reprint   : April   2017   Copies : 1000
5th Reprint   : April   2024   Copies : 500

Design & Layout :
Graaphic Design

Printed at :
Sudarsan Graphics Pvt. Ltd.,
4/641, 12th Link Street
3rd Cross Road, Nehru Nagar
Kottivakkam (OMR)
Chennai - 600 041

Contents

Preface   v

Key to Transliteration   vii

Talk 1   1
Objectivity is to face what is
without projecting ourselves into situations

Talk 2   10
Everything is explained in the wake of
understanding of what is

Talk 3   19
To be objective we need to understand the
reality of ourselves and what we experience

Talk 4   28
Whatever we see here or know is the
self-revealing, self-existent consciousness

Talk 5   38
The jagat is a manifestation, not a creation

Talk 6   48
Reality words - real, false, non-existent
and mithyā

Talk 7   59
Everything is sat-cit-ānanda

Preface

I gave a series of talks on objectivity calling it as 'yoga' for, I look upon objectivity as a means for self-growth. In fact, it brings Īśvara in one's life. It is so because what is empirically true is Īśvara. To be objective, one needs to be in harmony with what is. Therefore this is a very significant book with a meaningful title.

Ms. Sharon Cliff, a long time disciple of mine endowed with śraddhā and dedication, is responsible for quite a number of books. This book is also her loving contribution.

ॐ Dayananda.

Swami Dayananda Saraswati
Chennai
07 January 2010

KEY TO TRANSLITERATION AND PRONUNCIATION OF SANSKRIT LETTERS

Sanskrit is a highly phonetic language and hence accuracy in articulation of the letters is important. For those unfamiliar with the *Devanāgarī* script, the international transliteration is a guide to the proper pronunciation of Sanskrit letters.

अ	a	(b*u*t)		ट	ṭa	(*t*rue)*3
आ	ā	(f*a*ther)		ठ	ṭha	(an*th*ill)*3
इ	i	(*i*t)		ड	ḍa	(*d*rum)*3
ई	ī	(b*ea*t)		ढ	ḍha	(go*dh*ead)*3
उ	u	(f*u*ll)		ण	ṇa	(u*n*der)*3
ऊ	ū	(p*oo*l)		त	ta	(pa*th*)*4
ऋ	ṛ	(*r*hythm)		थ	tha	(*th*under)*4
ॠ	ṝ	(ma*ri*ne)		द	da	(*th*at)*4
ॡ	ḷ	(reve*lry*)		ध	dha	(brea*the*)*4
ए	e	(pl*ay*)		न	na	(*n*ut)*4
ऐ	ai	(*ai*sle)		प	pa	(*p*ut) 5
ओ	o	(g*o*)		फ	pha	(loo*ph*ole)*5
औ	au	(l*ou*d)		ब	ba	(*b*in) 5
क	ka	(see*k*) 1		भ	bha	(a*bh*or)*5
ख	kha	(bloc*kh*ead)*1		म	ma	(*m*uch) 5
ग	ga	(*g*et) 1		य	ya	(lo*y*al)
घ	gha	(lo*g h*ut)*1		र	ra	(*r*ed)
ङ	ṅa	(si*ng*) 1		ल	la	(*l*uck)
च	ca	(*ch*unk) 2		व	va	(*v*ase)
छ	cha	(cat*ch h*im)*2		श	śa	(*s*ure)
ज	ja	(*j*ump) 2		ष	ṣa	(*sh*un)
झ	jha	(he*dgeh*og)*2		स	sa	(*s*o)
ञ	ña	(bu*nch*) 2		ह	ha	(*h*um)

.	ṁ	anusvara	(nasalisation of preceding vowel)
:	ḥ	visarga	(aspiration of preceding vowel)
*			No exact English equivalents for these letters
ऽ	'	avagraha	(indicates a dropped vowel - not pronounced)
1.	Guttural	–	Pronounced from throat
2.	Palatal	–	Pronounced from palate
3.	Lingual	–	Pronounced from cerebrum
4.	Dental	–	Pronounced from teeth
5.	Labial	–	Pronounced from lips

The 5th letter of each of the above class – called nasals – are also pronounced nasally.

Talk 1

Objectivity is to face what is without projecting ourselves into situations

When I was a boy, eight or nine years old, studying in the village elementary school, my teacher told us how one should be through a vivid example. A wind storm can uproot trees because they do not bend, but it cannot uproot the reeds on the riverbank for they bend as the wind strikes. They do not resist the wind, so the wind cannot hurt them. They remain healthy. I remember this even today. We were told that we needed to be like those reeds and bend inside in response to a storm, to a howling wind of unpleasant situations and come back without breaking down. We bend to come back. We never say die.

Human life consists of both pleasant and unpleasant situations that we cannot avoid. They unfold in front of us day after day, unpleasant situations making us unhappy, and pleasant situations happy, even elated. How can we learn to bend so that we are not uprooted by these situations?

We have in the Bhagavad Gītā and its source book, the *upaniṣad,* wisdom that we can call the *Yoga of objectivity.* To be objective is to face what is. It means not projecting ourselves into situations. People hardly take things as they are but look at things in terms of how they should be—how their people should be; how other people should be even if they are not known to them. If the person is intimately connected to us, as siblings and so on, then we are very definite about how they should be. However, those persons are also very definite about how we should be. When this is the situation, relationships become one of high maintenance.

To be objective, we need to know that what is here is 'given'

To be objective, eyes and ears are not enough. We need minimum knowledge, knowledge of what is, and it has to be general. If we look at the syllabus of a medical school, we find that there is so much to learn about anatomy. In the first year, anatomy is the most difficult subject because the medical student has to remember unheard of Latin words. What is the need to study them? The students can plead for a syllabus consisting of diseases and remedies. But, if you are a general surgeon, you have to remember anatomy. You need to refer the anatomy book. Perhaps, one can practice medicine without knowing all about this body, but it is difficult to be objective without knowing the realities of living. We need to know that each one of us is living in a world that is not just out there always, but in a world that is often here in our head.

Īśvara-sṛṣṭi, the Lord's creation, means what is given, understanding which makes us objective. The sun is there, and it is able to send so much energy and light. How long does it take for the light of the sun to reach us here? What is its distance from the earth? We do not see the sun of 'now'. When we see the sun, we see the sun of eight minutes thirty two seconds ago because it takes on an average eight minutes thirty two seconds for its light to reach the earth. So, too, if we throw an object up, it comes down with increasing speed, thirty two feet per second per second. For a piece of wood to become fossilised, to become a stone, it takes millions of years. That is a geological reality. Similarly, we have forces, laws, means and ends that are given.

All that is here is given. There is Jupiter, Venus and Saturn. It was nice to see Saturn with its rings until I consulted an astrologer. Now that I know a little bit of astrology, I cannot see Saturn as Saturn because it is in the wrong place in my chart. However, that placement is also given. This is how truth is, but then, it elicits a response from me.

To be objective is to understand that there are many hidden variables beyond our control

Our perception of the world is conditioned by what it should have been, what it should be and should not be. It is how we look at the world. It is in our head. It would be nice to have a scorpion without a sting, but then it would not be a scorpion. A scorpion has a sting for its protection and survival, not to sting others. It would also be nice to have roses without thorns. We want the world to be to our liking. The head of the country should be different; he or she should act differently. Any policy decision, political or economic, is different from our thinking, while, for the others in the family, the decision is good and it should continue.

This 'should be' is inevitable. I find that a situation has to be reorganised or has to be changed so that I feel comfortable. It is what planning is, what execution is and it is what intelligent living is. I need to bring about desirable changes. I cannot say this is how it is and therefore let it be. No. That I need to bring about changes is not negotiable, and that I am not able to bring about all those changes that I want is a reality. How I respond to the reality, more often than not, is subjective, the agonies, the regrets, the frustrations, the ulcers. These are my own creations because I can be different. I need not undergo these inner upheavals. I can face things squarely and continue to be objective without subjecting myself to ups and downs, to 'yoyo' emotions. When I am objective to the world, I know that some changes need to be brought about that will make a difference in the lives of people.

Therefore, I do what I need to do, recognising that I am not in charge; I do not call all the shots. There are so many hidden variables, and I am not able to control all of them. I cannot control even a known variable, let alone hidden variables, and there are so many of them. It is imperative that

I learn a few things in order to be objective to the varying situations in life, pleasant and unpleasant. The sameness of mind towards the pleasant and unpleasant is said to be *yoga* in the Gītā.

To respond objectively, we need to draw on our inner strength, wisdom and attitude

We respond from our wisdom and our capacity to live by that wisdom. They are two different things, which is why we need *yoga*. If our response comes from wisdom alone, we do not need *yoga*. If it does not, then we have to fake it and make it, to use a popular expression. We have to subject ourselves to a way of living, cultivate a way of responding, and we have to have the wisdom to make that possible. Two things are important, gaining wisdom and living by that wisdom. It is *samacittatvam,* which means the sameness of response. In other words, there is no large variation in our response. To what? To pleasant and unpleasant situations, to acceptable and unacceptable situations. We can say, "No!" "Yes!" "Oh, no!" Three times we are allowed, but the fourth time we come back and draw on our wisdom. This called the practice of *yoga*.

As children, we played with Tanjore dolls like the one in my hand. (Swamiji holds up a small clay doll with a round bottom, painted like a king.) We brought it from India and kept it here for my classes. Look at it. The king is down; he lost his kingdom. The poor king. (Swamiji holds the doll down flat on the table; then lets it go. It rocks back and forth coming back up to its original upright position.) It has come up to be stable. There is a lot of wisdom in this doll. I put it on its back. It is finished. (Swamiji holds the doll down on its back; then lets it go. The doll rocks back and forth wobbling a little and then comes to a standstill in an upright position.) You are allowed to wobble a little bit, but then come back. That is called the practice of *yoga*.

We need to retain equipoise in the wake of what we like and dislike

You may hate something, but it is there. What are you going to do? Retain the same inner disposition, the equipoise, *nitya-samacittatvam*, in the wake of what you like and dislike, *iṣṭa-aniṣṭa-upapattiṣu*. *Iṣṭa* is what is liked. *Aniṣṭa* is what is disliked. *Upapattiṣu* means, 'when they happen/occur.' *Nityam* means 'always'.

Samacittatvam means 'retaining your poise, your composure,' without being carried away in elation or depression.

The Gītā does not give advice. If it gave advice, there need be only one page. Intelligent people do not need to be advised more than five or six times in life. Advice is easy. Everybody is a great advisor or philosopher when the problem belongs to somebody else. Anyone can give advice about what the other person should and should not do. However, when this person, who is a great advisor, has a problem, he or she then needs advice from others. We help each other without learning, but still, hearing our own words, we can learn a lot. We advice others, but following that advice ourselves is easier said than done. Then how do we get the inner disposition that bends and comes back, that does not stand stiff to get felled? How do we achieve that? There are background topics that give us the required strength and the wisdom. We will cover those topics, the areas that we are expected to know if we are to live a life of *samacittatvam*, which is *yoga*, the *yoga of objectivity*. The Gītā has seventeen chapters of discussion. A good part of these seventeen chapters deals with the background topic of what goes behind this *yoga* of inner composure and inner leisure. We will be looking into these topics in the next few sessions.

Talk 2

Everything is explained in the wake of understanding of what is

The reality of living is fraught with pleasant and unpleasant situations, which the *Gītā* accepts, it does not dispute this reality; there is no denial of problems. It wants us to reduce our subjectivity and increase our objectivity. I call it *yoga of objectivity*, which is the famous *karma-yoga*. We do not have an exaggerated value for things in the world, like money. It is assumed that money will solve all of our problems, but the truth is that it can also cause problems. Money does solve some problems, but to say that it solves all problems is not right. Money deserves a certain commitment; it does not come without a commitment unless it was earned in a previous birth. We accept continuity. One may inherit wealth by being born into a rich family. There should be some reason. We consider money to be Lakṣmī, and it is always earned. Therefore, there should be some commitment, but not total commitment, because there is a limit to what money can buy. It can buy a house, but it cannot make a home. It can buy books, but it cannot make one read them. Even if it can make one read, it cannot make one understand. Therefore, we say reduce subjectivity and increase objectivity by understanding that what we value may cause problems as well as solve problems. How else can you be objective?

A projection is called *adhyāsa, atasmin tad buddhiḥ. Tasmin tad buddhiḥ* means 'knowledge, perception of a given object as the object is.' This is a flower, and if we take it as a flower and not a mango, there is objectivity. In a given object (*tasmin*), there is the perception of that object as it is (*tad buddhiḥ*). If the object is a flower, we take it as a flower. *Buddhiḥ* means cognition. In the object 'flower,' there is 'flower' cognition. The perception results in our cognition of the flower and there is knowledge. Now, let us add one more word to the flower, an adjective, real flower. Why do we have to say that? Until all these artificial flowers came along, there was no need to use an adjective such as that. Now we need to use an adjective 'real'. There is a real flower, and there is a flower made of paper or plastic or silk and so on. Is this a real flower? It is a real flower that has been coloured. The stems were placed in coloured water which they absorbed. In today's world, there are virtual realities; therefore, we need to be more alert and informed. The responsibility on the part of a human being keeps on increasing because we do not know what is true and what is false. However, by understanding the background knowledge of certain critical topics, we can be objective to an extent.

Subjectivity is not due to wrong perception but due to wrong conclusion

The world, for each one of us, is I and everything else. Where do I draw the line between me and everything else? I draw the line where my nose ends. In other words, I do not exist where the extremities of my body ends. (Swamiji holds up two fingers, indicating the space in between). Here I do not exist. If a bullet were to pass in between my two fingers, I would have a topic to talk about for my lifetime.

"Did it hit you?"

"No."

"Then why are you talking like that?"

"It went right in between my fingers."

"Yes, I know, that is wonderful that something went in between your two fingers without touching you!"

"Thank goodness it did not touch me."

If the bullet went in between the person's fingers, he or she was untouched. However, the possibility of getting hit was very close, and that frightens the person. In psychotherapy, it is very real; it is legitimate fear which is very subjective.

Without denying anything, we shift the vision. Our perception may be right, but our conclusion may be wrong. We see the sun rise in the morning, our perception is not wrong. But a conclusion that the sun rises in the east, travels west, and returns to the east next morning is wrong. There is perception of the blue sky. The visual perception is not wrong, but the conclusion that there is a blue sky, as a ceiling of space, is wrong. The perception can be explained. So too, the perception of the twinkling stars appearing in the night and disappearing during the day can be explained. Whatever we see, which is not exactly what it appears to be, can be explained. That we are different from everything else and everything else is different from us can also be explained. Can we explain that away just as we can explain away the sunrise? We need not explain away the sunrise. If we travel to the North Pole during summer, we will see the sun going around us the whole day, and night lasts only half-hour or so. The visual perception of the sun going around us shows that it does not rise in the east and set in the west. There must be reasons for it. This is what enquiry is. We understand and appreciate that the earth is moving on its own axis, causing day and night, change of seasons and so on. Everything is explained in the wake of understanding of what is.

We have an erroneous notion that we are mortal insignificant beings

There is the notion that we are mortal insignificant beings who have a brief stay on this planet, and we try to make ourselves as comfortable as possible dealing with the existential issues. It is the 'poor-me' sentiment, me against the world. The world is not small, and what we are not is vast; and if we study a little astrophysics, just an article is enough, we will feel small.

Let us look at ourselves in the light of all that is here. (Swamiji holds up a picture of the comparative sizes of the planets and the sun). Looking at this picture, in the scheme of things, our solar system is a pinhead and Mother Earth is not even visible. Our sun itself is small compared to something else far bigger than that. Then when we think of the galaxies, where is our solar system, where is earth? Where is America? Where is Pennsylvania? Where is Saylorsburg? Where are we sitting? It is very healthy to look at it in this perspective.

We feel that we are insignificant. Just pick up one small rock from the roadside. If you ask the rock to tell its story, the rock would laugh at you,

"You want my story?"

"Yes."

"Do you have time to listen to my story?"

"How long is your story?"

"You would have to listen to me your whole lifetime; I have been around for millions of years. What I was before and how I became a rock is a geological story."

"Forget it; at most I have five minutes."

I have just given you a comparison to understand this 'I' in terms of time also.

We have a permanent Ninja stance, 'I against the world.' We are always on guard and need to be careful. Today, parents tell their children that if a stranger comes up and talks to them, they should scream and run away; and whole world is full of strangers. It is not very healthy to tell this to a child. Yet, they need to be told. Therefore, people have fear and a stance of fighting. The sense of persecution is there for everybody, that 'all are conspiring against me.' Everybody has a 'I-am-persecuted feeling,' and there is a reality about it. Then Vedanta comes along and tells us about what reality really is.

In the vision of Vedanta 'feeling insignificant' is only a point of view

I am the subject and everything else is object but my smallness and my insignificance is purely a point of view. It can be explained away, like the sunrise and the sunset, the blue sky, the flat earth, and the twinkling stars. The truth is 'I am the reality.' It is not another point of view, and it is not another reality. There is no other reality. There is only one reality, the reality that I am the whole. This is objectivity. That I am the whole is baffling and a tall claim, but it is true. Not only is it true, but there is also a methodology to unfold the fact.

We have issues with the world, how it should be and how it should not be. This is how we interact with the world, everyday. We hear some joke and laugh, or we listen to music that we love and are happy. The world is there and we are there. The world is the music that we confront. When that music catches our imagination, then that 'I', the demanding, complaining person, is resolved and the complaints are resolved. The world is and I am. Both are fused into one whole, and that wholeness is not unknown to us. It is known to us. Whether we are scanning the sky with a telescope and enjoying the stars, or we are looking through a microscope and admiring how the micro organisms live, we experience wholeness. In terms of experience, wholeness is understanding the fusion of this subject-object. All objects, including time and space, are nothing but the truth of me. How? There is one 'I' and there is the truth of 'I'. We will see this in the next talk.

Talk 3

To be objective we need to understand the reality of ourselves and what we experience

One needs to be alive to what is, alive to what is one's self, and to the reality of what one experiences. We know that there is no error in our perception. Then going one step further, we also know that even though there are no errors in one's perception there can be error in one's conclusion, which has already been discussed.

We mistake one object for another or one person for another. We commit mistakes in terms of a person's attributes. We also commit mistakes in terms of understanding ourselves and others. It is what psychology is. Many a good relationship is broken because there is an erroneous perception of the other. For a lot of people, love is control. "Don't I love you?" "Yes." "Then sit down." Unconditional love means one becomes vulnerable, and nobody wants to be vulnerable. The person has a need to be sure, so he or she has to operate within a defined area. Unless the person has control, he or she has a feeling that a relationship is impossible, which is why the person may end up relating to a drug addict or an alcoholic who needs to be taken care of. It is not out of love to take care of that person; it is a love to control that person. Taking care of means it should be general and one keeps giving.

The love to control is because of a childhood, growing up in a dysfunctional home. Perhaps there was an alcoholic parent at home, and therefore nothing was definite. It was all guesswork. Now the person is engaged in impractical relationships with no objectivity or pragmatism. It is endless. In such a situation, a person is not mistaken for another person, but the person is mistaken to be different from what he or she is. If the person is mistaken for another person, it is easy to rectify. One can show one's ID or social security card. It is not a problem. But when our pain and fear are projected onto another person, it is unfortunate.

It takes a lifetime to reduce subjectivity; you need to be comfortable being yourself. Therefore, I want you to relax and understand what I have to say because you may have a similar background, or you may come with a lot of preconceived notions. For a good part of your life, perhaps, you have made much emotional investment in certain beliefs, ideas and systems. You need not make effort to give up any of them, but they can remain suspended. Relax and listen. Let the openness of mind find what is.

To be objective is to understand that the subject and the object are one

The *upaniṣad* says that the self, the subject, is not separate from the self you need to know. You are there seeing me, hearing me. This is the reality, the seer, the seen, and the sight. Despite your confusion, the alignment of the seer, seen, sight is not variable. You are the seer, I am the seen, and both are connected by sight. The seer is the subject and the seen is the object. The subject is not variable whether one is hearer or speaker or any other, whereas the objects are variable, sound, touch, smell and so on, but all of them are 'object' to the subject 'I'. This is the reality, and if we want to be objective, we need to understand this reality. We cannot be objective without being alive to the reality of these two. These two are one reality in the vision of Vedanta. It is astounding because we have always known that the subject, the knower, is different from the known, the object, and that there are many objects and many subjects. How can it be said that the knower and the known are one?

To establish the prima facie possibility, in the *Upaniṣad* there is a statement: "Knowing which everything is known." It is a very big statement. Śvetaketu, who was twelve years old, was sent to stay with a teacher and study. At the age of twenty-four, after twelve years of Vedic study, he returned home. Śvetaketu was very proud; he could recite the whole Veda inside out. He was brilliant, and not only was he brilliant, he was conscious of the fact that he was brilliant. Learning does not include pride. One learns and remains humble. A person has learning but is ready to learn further from any source, even from a child. There is so much to learn.

Śvetaketu's father was upset. He called him and asked, "Śvetaketu, did you ask your teacher for that knowledge gaining which everything is known?" I translate it as, gaining which everything is 'as well known.' Uddālaka had asked Śvetaketu the question, seriously. Śvetaketu replied, "I do not think my teacher ever knew that." The answer again revealed his pride. What was his answer? 'Had he known, he would have taught me since I was the most brilliant student. Probably he did not know; therefore, he did not teach me.' Then Śvetaketu realised he had committed a mistake because he had not answered his father's question, "Did you ask for that knowledge?" He had not asked for that knowledge, so it would have been proper for him to have said, "I did not ask." He realised his mistake and then asked his father, "Is there such knowledge?" His father said, "Yes, there is such knowledge," and he cited a few examples to prove the existence of such knowledge.

Example of a clay pot helps one to understand the oneness of the subject and the object

Uddālaka said, *"ekena mṛtpiṇḍena sarvaṁ mṛṇmayaṁ vijñātaṁ syāt,* with (the knowledge of) one (*ekena*) lump of clay (*mṛtpiṇḍena*) all other things (*sarvam*) made of clay (*mṛṇmayam*) is known (*vijñātaṁ syāt*). By knowing one product of clay, like a pot, a jar, a lid, a vase, a plate, or a cup, all things made of clay become known. If there were a thousand forms of clay, each with a name, we would count one thousand pieces; but if we counted clay, there would be nothing more to count than just 'clay, clay, and clay.' By knowing what makes one clay pot, anything that is made of clay is as well known. One clay plus one thousand clay pots is equal to one. It is a different arithmetic. One plus one is one, and one plus a thousand is also one.

We use the word pot, so there must be an object for this word. I am confining myself to Upanisadic examples. (Swamiji holds up a clay pot.) If this pot had a human mind, it would have a lot of complaints. It took leave of its friends in India declaring, "I am going to America." The pot came here to be in America, and it ended up in an ashram under a table, complaining, "The Swami picks me up only occasionally. I have no job satisfaction. I have not seen America. Did I ever go to New York? No. I am sitting here in this dark place under the table." Thank Goodness, the pot does not have a human mind.

This is a pot according to all of you, and your understanding is that clay is an adjective and pot is a noun. Therefore, it is clay pot. Now, I share with you ancient knowledge, and I want to know where the pot is. In my hand? No, what is here in my hand is clay. Can you deny that? I say it is clay. Then where is your pot? In order to help you, I say, the weight of pot is the weight of clay. So you have a weightless pot. Further, the touch of pot is the touch of clay. All that is here is clay. Where is the pot? You cannot say it is on the clay. (Swamiji puts a flower on the clay pot.) This flower is on the clay. I can take the flower off, but I cannot take the pot off. The pot is not on the clay; it is not in the clay; and it is not off the clay. Where is the pot? This is ancient magic! I keep the pot right in front of you and make it disappear. I do not need to wear a full-sleeve shirt so that I can hide things up my sleeve like a magician does. Then what is the pot? You cannot say it does not exist because it holds water. Therefore, there is a pot; it is a reality. That is accepted. Now, if you accept the existence of the pot, then let us understand objectively what the pot is. To be objective is to give a status for this pot. I have to say it is neither existent, meaning it does not exist on its own, nor is it non-existent because it holds water. It will not hold water if there is a hole in it. So, while the pot is a reality, the status of the pot, the reality of the pot, the *ātmā* of the pot, the self of the pot, is clay.

The pot has its being in clay, yet the pot asks this question, "Swamiji, how can I get rooted in the knowledge I am clay?" "You need not get rooted, you are clay." It is a question of understanding. There is no necessity to get rooted. Words can keep you hooked on to the wrong notions. The pot **is** clay; the pot **was** clay, and the pot **will be** clay. It is clay even now. The pot is a value addition, an amazing addition that is miraculous. Without being there, it is there. That is what the miracle is, it should not be there on inquiry, but at the same time it should be there! The pot is magic.

Clay pot and clay vase are just words with their meaning

Now here is another clay object, a vase. It is also clay, but we have a different word for it. We have a problem. We cannot use the word pot because the pot form is different. This pot is clay, and the vase is clay. There are different words because there are different forms. The astounding part is that it is just a word sitting upon clay.

In the beginning, there was word, and the word was pot. In the beginning, it is all word, and the word's meaning is form, which is magic. **Form**

alone is magic. There is no magic in formlessness, which is why those who are critical of forms have not only lost the truth, but they have lost everything else. The form is contained in a name, in a word, and it is in your head. That is the beauty, and when a known word is spoken, the meaning transpires immediately. I want you to think of a pot, just a pot, without thinking of a substance. You are dealing with pots everyday. Your whole life is full of pots. "I love you" is one pot talking to another pot; one pot loves the other pot. Therefore, this is a very important topic. We do not know all about a pot, and yet we claim to be objective. I will talk more about this in the next talk.

Talk 4

Whatever we see here or know is the self-revealing, self-existent consciousness

The reality of any object is that it is neither self-existent nor non-existent. It is always in between, like a shirt. We cannot imagine a shirt without thinking of fabric at the same time. It is impossible. The truth, the *ātmā*, of the shirt is fabric; and if the shirt has to be sane and objective, it cannot afford to be ignorant of the fact, 'I am fabric.' The truth is that the shirt is fabric but the fabric is not shirt. However, knowing that it is fabric is not enough because there is the truth, the *ātmā*, of the fabric also. The fabric draws its being from yarn, and the yarn draws its being from fibres. So we have a series of words, shirt, fabric, yarn, fibre. We have four words in one shirt, meaning there are four objects without being objects. None of them has a being. Shirt has no being; fabric has no being; yarn has no being; fibres have no being; molecules have no being; atoms have no being; and particles have no being. Then what is the being? The *upaniṣad* says, "*yad idam sarvam ayam ātmā*, all that we know here is the self." We know either directly or indirectly through inference. All are the self.

You are the only person in the world you can refer to by the word I. You cannot use the word I for anybody else. Everyone and everything else is not I. What is not I? Whatever you objectify is not I. The sun is not I; the Milky Way is not I; the earth is not I; and everything else that is objectified, is not I.

The Milky Way exists, is. How do I know? It becomes evident to me. How does it become evident to me? It becomes evident to me through a means of knowing, which is why it is valid. There is a Milky Way, and there is our galaxy, which has billions of stars in it, our sun being one of them. The sun is evident to me, and the planets, Jupiter, Saturn, Mercury, Venus, Mars, each one of them either directly or indirectly is evident to me. The moon is evident to me, and that the earth has continents and its two-thirds is water, is evident to me. North America and South America are evident to me. Pennsylvania is evident to me. Saylorsburg is evident to me. So you keep saying, 'evident to me, evident to me.' Who is this me?

Does 'evident to me' mean it is evident to my body? If the body is I, then the body will not be evident to me, and I will never know that I have a body. No. There is a body; body is, and it is evident to me, particularly when I have a backache.

The body is evident to me, and any notion that I have about myself centred on my body, on my body condition such as I am fat, I am old, I am black, I am white, is also evident to me. The attributes of the body are evident to me. In fact, there is no body; there are only attributes. The body is like a pot. Body is a word, but I cannot think of the body without thinking of its limbs and other attributes. A bunch of cells makes up the body, and those cells can be reduced to something else. Then who is this I? Hunger and thirst are evident to me. Eyes and ears are evident to me. That the eyes see or that they do not see is evident to me, which is why the ophthalmologist checks with me. I ask him for a pair of glasses, and when he examines my eyes, he asks, "Do you see now?" I have to tell him whether I can see or not. Based upon what I say, he prescribes glasses. Therefore, I cannot say that I am the eyes or the ears, for they are evident to me.

Maybe my mind is I. No, the mind is variable and momentary. Mind means a thought, *vṛtti*, and a thought is momentary, which is why 'mind control' is meaningless, thoughts are too momentary to last. They go away. Although thoughts are momentary, they flow, and the object of those thoughts can be the same, like in a movie, which is evident to me. Without mind intervention, there would be no cognition. The flower you see in my hand is because there is a flower thought. The flower reflects light, and my eyes pick up the stimulus which is transferred into the image of the flower. It is called *vṛtti*, a thought. The very form of the object is the form of my thought, which I see; it is evident to me. I do not see anything other than what happens here in my mind. The universe may be vast, but the whole vastness is here in the mind, within these few inches of the head. So what occurs in my mind is evident to me. My knowledge is evident to me; my memories are evident to me; and that I am not able to recall, that I forget, is also evident to me; and, finally, my ignorance is evident to me. Any ignorance, anything that I do not know, is evident to me. So who am I? Time is evident to me; space is evident to me. Time and space are part of the whole thing, and the whole thing is evident to me. Every one of them exists, from ignorance onwards, because it is evident to me. Everything is because it is evident to me.

I do not need a means of knowing to know that I exist

Now, the question is, "The I, to whom everything becomes evident, is it existent or not?" I do not need a means of knowing to know that I exist. Ignorance is because I am witness to it; an emotion is because I am witness to it; hunger and thirst are because I am witness to them. I am aware of the hunger pangs because there is a means of knowing. With senses or without senses, I am able to objectify everything. Do I require a means of knowing to know that I exist? No, I am evident without requiring a means of knowing. I am the self, and the self is evident to itself. I am self-evident and self-revealing. If you understand exactly what is this evidence that I am talking about, you will understand what the nature of the self is. The self is self-evident, and everything else is evident to the self.

What does 'evident' mean? The Swami sitting here is evident to your eyes. What is that evidence; what is common in all that evidence, and what is the net result? There is Swami-consciousness. I will use one word, pot, pot consciousness; flower, flower consciousness; sun, sun consciousness; moon, moon consciousness; time, time consciousness; space/distance, space/distance consciousness; body, body consciousness; and the condition of my eyes, eye consciousness. There is ear consciousness, hunger consciousness, thirst consciousness, emotion consciousness, knowledge consciousness, memory consciousness, and ignorance consciousness.

What is invariable in all evidence is consciousness, the self, which is self-evident. It reveals itself, and it reveals everything else. In Sanskrit we use the word *samvit*, and in English we use the word consciousness which is only used relatively in such expressions as social consciousness, body consciousness, self-consciousness, unconsciousness, and sub-consciousness. We use the word consciousness in an unqualified sense. It is important to knock off the adjectives. Whether it is a Sanskrit word, an English word, it is more than just a word because its meaning is self-revealing. We need to knock off everything that it is construed to be, such as I am ignorant, I am mortal, I am this, and I am that. The whole set of notions centred on I, are conclusions that can be explained away. They are points of view.

The *Upaniṣad* says this consciousness, the *ātmā*, which is you, is the *ātmā* of everything.

"This is too much! *Ātmā* of everything?"

"Yes, everything means everything, heaven if there is one, and hell also if there is one."

"You say I am hell?"

"You are heaven, too."

"Both I am?"

"Yes, you are heaven and hell."

"How can I be both?"

"Maybe you are neither; only then can you be both."

What emerges from an inquiry into the words of the Upaniṣad is a sentence that I am going to talk about. Whatever we see or know here is consciousness, the self, *ātmā*. We say 'this' self, *ayam ātmā* because it is self-evident, and it never becomes 'that'. It is self-revealing *ayam ātmā.*

All that is here is magic because anything that you think of reduces itself to something else

In order to be objective, you need to know all that is here is consciousness, the self. What does 'all that is here' mean? All that is here is magic. There is nothing more than magic because any one thing that you think of reduces itself to something else. A lot of complex things are here. Take a seed of an orange tree, for example. Open the seed, and what do you see? A broken seed and whatever substance is there. Do you see any trace of the leaf, branches, trunk, flowers, fruit, or root system? No. Do you say a tree comes from this seed, where there is no trace of any of its parts? It is true; a tree comes from its seed. If none of these parts was there, how can the orange tree come from it? If they were not there, then any seed could produce an orange tree. Any seed could produce anything. In fact, you would not need a seed. But that is not so. From the orange seed, an orange tree comes. Then the tree is there. Yes, a tree must be there. How? In the form of software! The orange tree is there unmanifest and undifferentiated. It is pure knowledge. In the seed, the tree is only a word, knowledge. It is software. In the seed is knowledge of the tree. It is not buried and so on. It is all knowledge. You can understand that and because you can understand, it is called knowledge. In the seed, invisible and undifferentiated, lies the knowledge of the tree that is to come with all the differentiation. Then what happens? Given time, place and the right conditions, the tree and the oranges will come.

Now, let us look at an orange leaf. What is a leaf? Is the chlorophyll a leaf? No. Is the cellulose a leaf? No. What is a leaf? Again, it is knowledge. Leaf is a word, knowledge. Leaf remains knowledge in the seed. It is manifest knowledge. Again, the orange is knowledge. What is the orange? Is colour the orange? Orange is a word that carries some knowledge. What is juice? It is again reducible to water, sugar, etc. It is reduced to so many things. Again, what is water? Water is just a word, it is H_2O. What is hydrogen? Again, it is just a word. They are all words. Word means meaning and meaning is knowledge. What is a branch? What is a twig? What is a trunk? What is a root?

What is earth? The whole thing is knowledge. Before manifest knowledge, there was unmanifest knowledge. That is all that is here. Where knowledge is, there consciousness is because there cannot be knowledge without consciousness. It is all one consciousness.

In Sanskrit, there is one word, *jagat*, and there is no equivalent for it. *Jagat* means the world we come across, plus our own body, mind, and senses, which also we come across. All of that together is called *jagat*, one word. In the beginning, there was word, *jagat*, and the word was with God. There seems to be a lot of knowledge in all this. It is like a flower unfolding. We will see further what is there in all these words in the next talk.

Talk 5

The jagat is a manifestation, not a creation

According to scientists, the entire *jagat*, including my body-mind-sense complex, is a manifestation and not a creation. Manifestation means what is unmanifest comes to manifest, just as a tree, in the form of unmanifest knowledge in a seed, comes to manifest, given time and place. An undifferentiated tree in the seed is the knowledge of the unmanifest tree.

Scientists say that fourteen billion years or so ago, the entire universe was a soup of matter. It was so hot that the immutable forces, the strong force (the nuclear force), the gravitational force, the electromagnetic force, and the weak force, were unmanifest. Let us look at today's language. It says unmanifest, and Vedanta also says *avyaktam*, unmanifest. The forces were not allowed to operate because the temperature was so high. It is like the water in the ocean that does not freeze in winter due to the presence of salt, which lowers the freezing point. A similar thing happened with the *jagat*. Because of the extraordinarily high temperature, the immutable forces were muted; they were made inoperable, could not do anything. Then the temperature went down. Why? Scientists will say they do not know. If the temperature did not go down, there would be no manifestation. But it did go down; and as the temperature went down, the strong force became active and first created quarks. Then there is a whole story of the other forces coming together to see this universe manifest.

The question is, was it a random movement or was it a methodical progression to the end in view, the universe as it is now. If the various things that happened did not happen the way they did, there would be no universe. The scientists know this. It is like alphabet soup that contains the letters A B C and so on, from which words can be made. Before taking the soup, the children play with the edible letters by making words. Take the word 'universe'. What is the probability of the letters assembling themselves into the word 'universe' with the word for each of its constituents? The probability is just nil; it is zero probability. When we study the scientists' theory, they say if this or that had not happened, there would be no universe. This much they know. So the whole universe, with further possibilities, is not closed. A star may burn itself out to become a black hole, and a new star may be born. All these stars are important to maintain the temperature of the universe; otherwise it will collapse. All that is here is a manifestation, and manifestation means it was here before, but in an unmanifest condition; then it came to manifest.

All that is here was, before *sṛṣṭi*, non-separate from that one reality, *sat*, knowing which everything is as well known.

Remember what I said previously from the *Upaniṣad*, "Knowing which everything is as well known." Śvetaketu asked his father, "Is there such knowledge?" His father, Uddālaka, told him that by understanding the truth of one clay pot, the truth of all earthenware would be known. Uddālaka then gives another example. If there are many gold ornaments, understand what one gold ornament is. The weight of a gold chain is the weight of gold; its shine is the shine of gold; its strength is the strength of gold. So the shine, weight, strength and malleability of the gold chain belong to gold. If we know that the truth of the gold chain is the truth of gold, we have understood the entire world of gold ornaments, the entire world of gold. All that is there is gold. If we count gold, that is it. There are one million ornaments all made of gold; and, if we count gold, there is nothing more to count. There is only one, gold.

Śvetaketu was convinced. He addressed his father, "Please teach me all about this knowledge." Therefore, there is one more beginning. *Sat eva saumya idam agre āsīt ekam eva advitīyam*, my dear Śvetaketu, all that is here was before, non-separate from the non-dual *Sat*, reality. The entire *jagat* was one *vastu*, non-dual reality. When we say one, it has no definiteness. One is subject to becoming many; one is subject to becoming a fraction; one can be a half; and one can be added, one plus one is equal to two. There is one universe, but many galaxies. There is one galaxy, but millions of stars, therefore systems. There is one sun, but many planets. There is one planet Earth, but many continents. There is one continent, but many countries. There is one country, but many states. There is one state, but many counties. There is one county, but many townships. There is one township, but many houses. There is one house, but many rooms. There is one body, but there are ten fingers and millions of cells. "I give up." "Yes, give up this stand." "Okay, what is this one?" There is one non-dual, one without a second. We cannot count further.

There is only the Whole

These one million ornaments came from one tonne of gold. It was one tonne gold, and it remains as one tonne of gold. This is what is said by "*pūrṇam adaḥ pūrṇam idam pūrṇāt pūrṇam udacyate pūrṇasya pūrṇam ādāya pūrṇam eva avaśiṣyate*, that was whole; this is whole. From that whole, this whole came. Knowing this whole as that whole, the whole remains." We may get confused, but, with understanding, it becomes meaningful. It was one tonne of gold, and remains one tonne of gold, but it is not just gold. It has become varieties of ornaments, bangles, chains, and different rings like nose rings, and earrings. There are one million ornaments, and they all came from one tonne of gold. We do not need to melt the ornaments to find out all that is there is gold. The truth of these one million ornaments is one tonne of gold. Similarly, all this before it came to manifestation was non-dual *Sat*; then, when it came to manifestation, *Sat* continues to be here. What is the difference? Non-dual one plus many is still non-dual one. One plus space, one plus time, one plus galaxies is still the non-dual one. It was one; it is one. This is the famous line: "It is one, and it is non-dual, *ekam eva advitīyam*." What came of that one includes our body-mind-sense complex. This is the truth.

The following is an example of how it can be seen erroneously. It was one non-dual; then it became many. Therefore, every individual has one divine spark, a speck of that one reality. So you are a speck, I am a speck, and the realisation is 'I am a speck.' Previously, you thought you were somebody, a small, big person. At home at least you were popular. Now, after all these spiritual pursuits, what did you discover? 'I am a speck, but a divine speck.' You call yourself a speck, and then you put some adjective in front of it, 'I am a divine speck.' No. The teaching is, just as gold became the chain and the bangle, but remains as gold, *Sat* remains one, non-dual.

We need to be taught that we are one non-dual self-shining consciousness

Imagine that the chain and the bangle are given a human mind. We require a human mind since it can pick up complexes. Let us suppose that the bangle is jealous of the chain because it is remote from the heart of the person; whereas, the chain is always close, and enjoys the warmth of the person.

The bangle thinks, "Look at my lot. I am open to the sun and rain. Once upon a time, I was a shiny new bangle, but now I have so many scratches because this woman frequently washes her hands. At this rate I will soon be gone. I wish I were a chain." However, the chain has its own problems. The chain feels, "I have no job satisfaction, nobody looks at me. When winter comes, I am lost. I cannot be seen because they wear so many clothes. I cannot breathe fresh air or enjoy the sun. Look at the bangle. It is always available for public appreciation. I wish I were a bangle."

Now, let us suppose their prayers were answered. The bangle became the chain and the chain became the bangle. And they retained the knowledge of their previous lives. What was previously the chain now thinks, "Ahhh, I am now a bangle, wonderful." Then, when the woman washes her hands, it complains, "What! Is this how you treat me as a bangle? Do you know that I was a chain before?" The chain also would have the same problem. Both the bangle and the chain require to be taught, "Before you were born, you were gold; you came to manifest and were called bangle and chain, but you are gold. Each one of you has a role to play and a purpose to serve. There is a name, and with that name you are recognised, which we call form. Form is just a word with its meaning. It is not a tangible object. The *ātmā* of the chain is the *ātmā* of the bangle, the *ātmā* of the ring also."

Therefore, the one million ornaments, if they have a human mind, have to be taught, "From out of which you all came, by which you are all sustained, and unto which you all go back, that gold, that self-shining gold you are, *tattvamasi*." As the chain was taught, it was surprised to hear that it is really big, it asked:

"Am I gold? Really?"

"Yes, and the other ones are also gold, all gold, gold, gold; and you are free to be a chain."

It is just an example which has its own limitations.

The *jagat*, with its names and forms, is non-separate from the self-evident being. The self-evident being lends its existence to everything. 'Everything' is but words with their meanings, nothing tangible. Whether it is time and space or anything in time and space, nothing has any being except the one being that is you. Therefore, one non-dual *Sat* alone was here before. Even now that one non-dual *Sat* alone is here.

"That one *Sat* alone is here?"

"Yes."

"Where is that?"

"Hey, that is what you are."

"Me?"

"Yes."

"What, me?"

"Self-evident you."

"Self-evident me? I am that?"

"Yes."

"All of these are me?"

"Yes."

"But did I create all of them?"

"In a way, yes; and in a way, no."

We will see what this yes and no mean in the next talk.

Talk 6

Reality words - real, false, non-existent and mithyā

We need a word, a word that conveys the reality of an object that we call real, without enquiry. A pot is real. And the knower of the pot is also real. The knower-known reality is to be understood in terms of our total vision of what is. The pot can be told that it is clay and the chain can be told that it is gold, but then the reality of seer-seen and knower-known has to be assimilated, and that assimilated knowledge is revealed by a reality word.

When we say that the pot is real, we have used up the word real in covering the pot. Our understanding is that time is real, space is real, the sun is real, and the various laws that are here are real. We take everything as real, and there are so many real things in the world. To be objective is to deal with real things, not shadows, not fancies, and not our imagination or projections. Things need to be reduced to realities. Therefore, we have reality words like real, false, and non-existent. We take any simple thing, like a pot, or any complex thing like a computer, as real. Our understanding is that a flower, a leaf, and a thought are all real things.

Then what is false? What we see in our dream is false. In the dream, the jackpot that one wins is false. We also come across certain statements that are false, such as water is H_2O, that are not true. So we have to use a word to convey what is not true and we use the word false. Then there is the word non-existent and the example for that is a square circle or a circular square.

These three words, true, false, and non-existent, are used to cover our understanding of the realities of living. We think we will be objective if we go by what is real. It is false, because we are not objective. We do not have an adequate reality-word for pot. We have already used up the word real for covering the pot which is not true. We understand that the pot is not false, the pot is not non-existent, and the pot does not exist by itself.

Pot is just a word for a form

When we hear the word pot, immediately a form comes to our mind. We cannot think of a pot without thinking of something else, because pot is just a word for a form. Form is the meaning of the word pot. In books in English on Vedanta, we come across words such as illusion and delusion which have the same meaning as false. The pot, however, cannot be dismissed as unreal or as an illusion or as a delusion. The pot is not false, much less non-existent, but is it real? If it is real, then when we see the pot, why do we always see the substance, which in this case is clay? Why are we not able to see the pot without seeing the substance? If the pot is real, we should be able to see it without seeing the substance. To see the pot, we need not see the flower; and to see the flower, we need not see the pot. They are different objects. But then in order to see the pot, we need to see the substance, and here, in our example, it is clay. We cannot even imagine a pot without thinking of a substance. As I mentioned earlier, the pot is not sitting on clay; it is not in the clay; and it is not off the clay. The pot is clay. Because of our training, we assume that if the pot is clay, the clay must be pot, but that is not true. The clay is not always a pot; the clay can be just a clod, an ant-hill.

It can be a lump; it can be powder; it can be a lid; it can be a cup; or it can be a pot. It can be anything. Clay is clay; it is not a pot. We also cannot say that wherever there is a pot, there is clay. It is not true. Wherever there is a pot there can be different substances, like brass, copper, tin and so on. Therefore, it is clear that clay is clay; it is not a pot. However, a clay pot draws its being from clay. If we say the pot is, the 'is-ness' belongs to clay. If the clay were taken away, there can be no pot. We cannot bring a clay pot without bringing clay. It is impossible, which means, in this case, we must use the word 'real' for the clay, the reality that is there. Clay is the reality of the pot. Therefore, the word real is taken away from the pot to cover our understanding of clay. The clay is real. Then our thinking is that if the pot is not real, it must be false. We have pendulum-like thinking. The pot is not false because it holds water. So, the pot is not false; it is not non-existent, but it is not real either.

What is our understanding of the pot in terms of reality? We have a Sanskrit word, but we need an English word. We cannot say the pot is a delusion or an illusion. We can only say that the pot is not non-existent, nor is it false, *asat. Asat* means non-existent, false, and *sat* means real. The pot is neither *sat* nor *asat.* Then what is the pot? *Sadasadbhyām anirvacanīyam,* that which cannot be categorically stated as real (*satyam*) or false, non-existent (*asatyam*), but which is called, in one word, *mithyā.* In order to be objective, we must understand the pot in terms of its reality. When we understand that the pot is neither real nor false nor non-existent, but that it is *mithyā,* we can deal with it. After all, we are always after the real thing, and whatever we deal with, including our own body, is neither real nor false.

The one invariable being, consciousness, is satyam

The ocean, the lake, and tears draw their reality from water. There cannot be tears without water. From many different standpoints, water is the reality; and it can be in the form of a river, wave, pond, lake, bay, sea, or an ocean.

If the Indian Ocean wave were to tell an Atlantic Ocean wave, "You are the ocean."

How would the Atlantic Ocean wave assimilate this knowledge? The Atlantic Ocean wave would say,

"Come on, what are you talking about?"

The Indian Ocean wave would reply, "You are the ocean. You are born of ocean, sustained by and resolve into the ocean."

"Even then how can I be the ocean? I am only a wave."

"Yes, *mithyā* wave-ness and *mithyā* ocean-ness, both are *mithyā* attributes of water. You are water. As water, you can say 'Ocean I am,' 'Wave I am.' So too, Īśvara I am, the self, the consciousness. Individual *jīva* I am, the self, the consciousness. The difference is *mithyā*."

You are that, *tattvamasi,* is the final equation in the world. There are many equations, but this is the ultimate one. It cannot be improved upon any further. When the wave is told, "You are the ocean," the wave cannot accept it. The wave wants to walk away, but it cannot walk away because it wants to be the ocean, "I wish that it were true, but then the sad part is that it is not true; the wave is not the ocean." The wave has to be led through the steps of inquiry to appreciate that wave is a word for which there is a form and that one cannot think of a wave without thinking of water. The top of the wave, the middle of the wave, the entire wave is but water. Therefore, the *ātmā*, the reality of the wave is water.

Now let us look at water, the reality of the ocean. Can you think of the ocean without thinking of water? No, you cannot. However, water is not the ocean; water is H_2O. Three atoms are there in water. There is only one reality, but there are three words, *sat*, *cit*, and *ānanda*. The word is *sat-cit-ānanda*.

Therefore you can say, 'I am Īśvara.' But only in a Vedanta classroom can you say so. Elsewhere, you would be construed as a crazy person. Once, I was to catch my flight at the Toronto airport when this Hare Kṛṣṇa person came up to me wanting to sell a book. I said very politely, '*Namaskar*' and moved along. He followed me and asked, "To which *sampradāya* do you belong?" I said something and moved on, and again he

followed me and said, "You are not Īśvara."
I answered, "That is why I am catching a flight!"

Consciousness is non-negatable, limitless, invariable, self-revealing vastu

Somebody asked the other day, "What is consciousness?" Consciousness is a word that is generally qualified, for example, when you see me, there is Swami consciousness. When you hear me, there is word-meaning consciousness. When there is sight, there is colour-and-form consciousness, this is red, orange, a cube, round and so on. When there is smell, there is smell consciousness, rose fragrance, jasmine fragrance. So there is rose-fragrance consciousness, jasmine-fragrance consciousness. Then when there is taste and touch, hot, cold, it is hot consciousness and cold consciousness. Any object that you infer, there is that inferred-object consciousness. This is knowledge.

Generally, when you hear a word, its meaning transpires in your mind. I am going to give you an exercise here. Close your eyes, and see the meaning of the words I say. Apple. Orange. Fruit.

Orange tree. Crow. Dog. Elephant. Camel. Table. Chair. Book. Pen. Car. Consciousness. Consciousness. Consciousness. See the meaning. Consciousness. Book. Book consciousness. Pen. Pen consciousness. Chair. Chair consciousness. Elephant. Elephant consciousness. Consciousness. Your body height. Body-height consciousness. Weight. Weight consciousness. Colour. Colour consciousness. Age. Age consciousness. Consciousness.

Now open your eyes. What did you see when I said table consciousness? There was consciousness plus an object. There is no table without your being conscious of it. Chair. There is chair consciousness. Consciousness is invariable. When the word is consciousness, you cannot say consciousness is an object. Consciousness is not an object like a table. At the same time, there is meaning for the word consciousness, and the meaning is not an object. If it is not an object, then what is that? It is you, just you.

Consciousness is *satyam*. It has no height and no width. It has no limit whatsoever, vertically or horizontally. Consciousness is spatially limitless; it is not located in space. There is space consciousness, and there is time consciousness;

but, consciousness itself is neither bound by space nor time. It is space-wise, time-wise limitless. This is what we experience whenever we are happy. This limitlessness is what we call *ānanda*. It is what water is for the wave. The ocean is water, and the wave is water. Therefore, the sentence "You are that, *tattvamasi*" is meaningful. This *jagat* is non-separate from that cause from which it has come to manifest. It is an intelligent manifestation, and this *jagat* is *mithyā*. Remember where there is *mithyā*, there is *satyam*.

Consciousness, the truth, can never be covered because it happens to be you

When we say that the pot is *mithyā*, then there is *satyam* all over. Somebody said, "Behind the veil of *mithyā* there is *satyam*." (Swamiji holds up a clay pot). The pot does not have a veil over clay. The pot does not and cannot cover the clay. *Satyam* is revealed. What is the truth can never be covered because it happens to be you, consciousness. How can it be covered? It is *satyam*. If I am *satyam*, consciousness is *satyam*.

All knowledge-consciousness, Īśvara, is because of some *mithyā upādhi*, adjunct. Similarly, limited knowledge-consciousness is because of individual *mithyā upādhi*. We will look into this in the next talk.

Talk 7

Everything is sat-cit-ānanda

The entire *jagat* is given and it is from *sat-cit-ānanda*. The objective perception, *mithyā*, is different from any subjective perception. But, who created this objective *mithyā*? We know that a rope is created by an intelligent being, even though we do not see him or her. Then, who created this body, hands, and mind? Our body is given. Nobody has any knowledge of how exactly this body was created and yet there is so much knowledge involved. Neither our mother, our father, our grandparents, nor the primitive man had any knowledge of this body to put it together. Therefore, who created this body? The body is given. It is from *sat-cit-ānanda*.

Mithyā is knowledge of forms. A table is a form, and wood is another form. The wood can be reduced to pulp, which can be reduced further. All that is here is knowledge, and this knowledge is also *mithyā*. What kind of *mithyā*? It is not subjective because there is valid knowledge involved. Therefore, it is objective *mithyā*, which is empirically true. Subjectivity is not empirically true, but it is also *mithyā* in Sanskrit language.

Let us take any knowledge, knowledge of a flower, for instance. The whole mind is occupied by this flower. The flower is an object of our thought. Whether it is a small object or a big object, the mind has a thought. If we see a mustard seed, it is not that the mustard seed occupies only one corner of our mind, it occupies the whole mind. The mustard seed is the object of thought. (Swamiji holds up a flower). When we see this object and we have a thought, then we have knowledge, knowledge of the flower. What is the truth of this flower knowledge? There is colour knowledge, there is petal knowledge, and there is stem knowledge. By reducing the flower to its own constituents, we understand what *mithyā* is.

Now, let us imagine that I remove these petals one by one. One petal is not a flower; another petal is not a flower; another petal is not a flower, and another petal is not a flower. Where the flower? The pollen is not flower, and the stem is not a flower. Where is the flower? The flower is gone. This is called Vedanta magic. Honestly, you take any one thing, flower or a petal, it is knowledge. And flower knowledge is consciousness. It is *saccidānanda*. The flower is *saccidānanda*; the petal is *saccidānanda*; the colour is *saccidānanda*; the stalk is *saccidānanda*; and space-time in which they all exist is *saccidānanda*. The flower knowledge and also the memory of the flower is *saccidānanda*. There is a lot of knowledge involved in this *mithyā* flower. One can spend a lifetime as a scientist studying a flower. Why does this flower have this form with this type of petal? Why does the other flower have a different type of petal? Our knowledge is limited; it extends up to one more question. However, there is one thing that we know. We know that there is so much knowledge involved. The flower is knowledge, which is *mithyā*. That knowledge must be there in the same *saccidānanda* because, being *mithyā*, it is not other than *saccidānanda*. While *saccidānanda* is not flower knowledge or petal knowledge, both are *saccidānanda*.

Knowledge of the jagat is mithyā

Knowledge of the entire *jagat*, including our body-mind-sense complex, is *mithyā*, and it is

never separate from *sat-cit-ānanda*. *Sat-cit-ānanda*
with all-knowledge and all-power is Īśvara, the
Lord. When we say Śiva, the Lord, there is always
the power, *śakti*. The Lord with that *māyā-śakti*,
with reference to the *jagat*, is all-knowledge.
Before this manifestation, there was unmanifest
all-knowledge, like in a seed. The whole tree,
which is knowledge, is unmanifest in the seed. All-
knowledge unmanifest is Īśvara, and again when
it is manifest, it is all-knowledge, which is Īśvara.
That is why it is available for us to know.

All that is here is a manifestation of Īśvara's knowledge

All that is here is all-knowledge which is
saccidānanda. This is what we say *īśvara-sṛṣṭi*,
Īśvara's creation. All that is here is a manifestation
of Īśvara's knowledge. "In the beginning, there
was word." Let us add here that word means *jagat*,
just one word. In the beginning, there was word,
jagat, and the word was with God, Īśvara, and
the word was God. True. Then God is what?
Saccidānanda, essentially. *Saccidānanda* is not word,
but word is *saccidānanda*. Word is God. Word is its
meaning. If there is no meaning for a word, it is not

a word; it is a group of sounds, like *gagaba*. What is *gagaba*? *Gagaba* is *jabaga*. What is *jabaga*? *Gagaba*. A meaning must be there.

Jagat is a word, one word, and it should be only one word. I am happy that it is only one word. There is no plural, it is singular. 'Flower' is a singular word. But within the word 'flower' we find there are so many words such as petal, stamen, pollen and so on. We say therefore Īśvara is all-knowledge manifest in the form of this *jagat*; and it is available for knowledge. How do we assimilate this? It is like the experience of our dream.

The dream world is a manifestation of myself

Whether or not a dream is an open letter with certain messages for you, the dream is a great blessing. Otherwise, it is not easy for anybody to understand Īśvara. In deep sleep, you have no knowledge of the world. You are consciousness, *saccidānanda*, but you are not all-knowledge. In fact, you are all-ignorance. Then you wake up halfway, which means you are not alive to your physical body or to the external world. You are dreaming. Suppose you dreamt that you went for a hike up the hill and fell down. You fractured your leg, and was not able to move. Three days went by, and there was nobody around, and you were starving. The dream itself was due to a heavy six-course dinner you ate before going to bed. But in the dream, you created a new world where you did not eat at all, which means that what was in your stomach had no relevance.

In your dream, you thought of the sun, and the sun was there in time and space. You did not create time and space separately and then put the sun there. This is how the creation is and it is also what time and space are. You thought of the sun, and the sun came along with time and space. This is how it is. You can get French fries without catsup, but you cannot get the sun without time and space. You thought of the sun, and the sun was there. You thought of the earth, and the earth was there. You thought of the mountains, and the mountains were there. You thought of the trees, of the birds, of horses, of people, and all of them were there! And you create a body for yourself.

In the dream one person complains, "This world is too much with me; it is *saṁsāra.*" Vedanta does not say that. Vedanta says that the whole world is fullness, *saccidānanda*, not bondage. Then another person says, "This world is filled with sorrow and pain, *duḥkha*, life is *duḥkha*, birth is *duḥkha*, death is *duḥkha*." Vedanta does not see it that way, but then one person in the dream says it is all *duḥkha*. It is called conditioning. Yet another person says, "We cannot get total pleasure here in this world because we are mortals, and we have limitations. There is pain and sorrow here, but we can go to paradise after death where we will have unlimited objects and pleasures, so, let us go to paradise." In fact, the most dangerous thing for a human being, for humanity and for the world, is the surrender of one's reasoning. This allergy to reasoning is a very, very sad thing. Here is another example, "My husband is so intellectual that he is always functioning from the left side of his brain, not the right side." We need the left side and right side as well.

Everyone in your dream looks at that world in his or her own way. "The creator of the world is in heaven, and Father in heaven created the world." Then there is the guru stuff. One guru says, "Surrender everything to me, your mind, your body, your wealth, and I will give you freedom, *mokṣa*." Then there is another who sounds more rational. He says, "The guru is only a signpost pointing out *mokṣa*, and there are many pitfalls on the way; you must walk carefully." Really speaking, you are the very nature of *mokṣa*. We are not solving a problem here. I am making you see that there is no problem. So, you have different people in your dream, and you have created them all.

Now, who is the maker of the dream? I am. My knowledge of sun is the sun; my knowledge of time is time; my knowledge of space is space. My knowledge is everything that is there. The dream is nothing but knowledge. Where am I in the dream? The whole *jagat* is a manifestation of my self. What does my 'self' mean? It is *Saccidānanda*. But not just *saccidānanda*; that will not make a complex world like the dream. It is *saccidānanda* plus knowledge, plus power, and then I manifest. This is the dream. And when I wake up, I am in the world of Īśvara, *Saccidānanda* plus knowledge, plus power.

I am the same *saccidānanda* when awake, and Īśvara is also *saccidānanda*. *Saccidānanda* is what counts and it is only one, non-dually one. Īśvara is *saccidānanda* with knowledge and power accounting for the entire *jagat*, known and unknown, including my body, which is not properly known to me. How it is put together and what is there is not completely known to me. The brain is still being mapped out. There is knowledge involved, such as biology, physiology, pathology, psychology, epistemology, physics, and there is *dharma* and *karma*. All this knowledge is there.

A person is objective when he or she can say I am connected, highly connected. Connected to whom? To Īśvara. The physical world is Īśvara, and we are a part of that physical world. There is a physical order, and the physical order pervades us. The physical order reveals the presence of Īśvara. When we raise our hand, it is Īśvara's physical order; and if sometimes it does not raise when we order it to, that is also Īśvara's order. We are always in Īśvara's presence with the physical, biological, and psychological orders. Hunger, thirst, old-age pains, and everything else is given, and it is all within the order. Illness and the capacity to correct that illness are given and both are within the order. We have to make use of that. Every emotion is within Īśvara's order, including jealousy, hatred, and fear. It is the psychological order, and there is a reason for it. If we have fear, welcome it. If we are not afraid of fear, we are objective. We need to be kind to ourselves. "I hate myself." "Why?" "I do not like my emotions." "Why don't you like your emotions?" "Because I do not like them." The dislike is pure emotion, and it is also part of the order. It has a background. We must accept the order, including our dislike; then we will have a reason to like it.

To be objective is not to get rid of subjectivity, but to see Īśvara's presence in the subjectivity

Everything is in order. *Dharma* is order and *karma* is order. "Why do I have these parents?" It is due to *karma*, which is within the order. "Why did I have that childhood?" We do not know why, and we need not question that. Some order is there. Whatever is there is there for many reasons, including the parent's *karma* and one's own. It is endless. Therefore, to be objective is not to get rid of subjectivity, but to see Īśvara's presence in the subjectivity. It is Vedanta, to be objective all the way. We see our guilt and our hurt within the order of Īśvara.

All that is here is order, one great order that is Īśvara. All-knowledge is all-order, and we are connected to the order. Any which way we look at ourselves, we are connected, highly connected. This knowledge makes us objective. If we live in this awareness of the presence of Īśvara, I would say, it is *Yoga of Objectivity*.

Oṁ Tat Sat

For a list of our other publications,
please visit the website at:
www.avrpt.com

...or contact :

ARSHA VIDYA RESEARCH
AND PUBLICATION TRUST
4 Sir Desika Road,
Mylapore Chennai 600 004
Ph   : 044 - 2499 7131
Email   : avrandpt@gmail.com
Website : www.avrpt.com

ARSHA VIDYA GURUKULAM
Anaikatti P.O.
Coimbatore 641 108
Ph   : 0422 - 2657001
Fax   : 0422 - 2657002
Email   : office@arshavidya.in
Website : www.arshavidya.in

SWAMI DAYANANDA ASHRAM
Swami Dayananda Nagar
Muni-Ki-Reti
Rishikesh, Uttarakhand 249 201
Ph   : 0135 - 2430769
Email   : ashrambookstore@yahoo.com
Website : www.dayananda.org

ARSHA VIDYA GURUKULAM
P.O. Box 1059. Pennsylvania
PA 18353, USA
Ph   : 001 - 570 - 992 - 2339
Email   : avp@epix.net
Website : www.arshavidya.org

ARSHA VIDYA TIRTHA
R-17 Yudhishthir Marg, Behind Secretariat
C scheme Jaipur. 302005
Ph   : 0141 2228766

Our publications are also available at all leading bookstores and
downloadable through the 'Teachings of Swami Dayananda'
APP for Android and Apple devices.